Find the Insect

By Cate Foley

Welcome Books

Children's Press
A Division of Grolier Publishing
New York / London / Hong Kong / Sydney
Danbury, Connecticut

Photo Credits: Cover, p. 9, 11, 21 © Donald Specker/Animals Animals; p. 5, 7, 21 © Michael Fogden/Animals Animals; p.13, 15, 21 © Michael Habicht/Animals Animals; p.17, 19, 21 © Index Stock Imagery

Contributing Editor: Jennifer Ceaser
Book Design: MaryJane Wojciechowski

Visit Children's Press on the Internet at:
http://publishing.grolier.com

Library of Congress Cataloging-in-Publication Data

Foley, Cate.
    Find the insect / by Cate Foley.
        p. cm. — (Hide and seek)
    Includes bibliographical references and index.
    Summary: Shows how different kinds of insects, including moths, an inchworm,
        a ladybug, and a grasshopper, are able to blend into their surroundings.
    ISBN 0-516-23096-4 (lib. bdg.) — ISBN 0-516-23021-2 (pbk.)
    1. Insects—Juvenile literature. 2. Camouflage (Biology)—Juvenile literature. [1. Insects.
2. Camouflage (Biology) I. Title.
QL467.2.F65 2000
    595.7—dc21   00-024582

Contents

1 An Insect with Wings   4

2 An Inchworm   10

3 A Red Insect   12

4 A Grasshopper   18

5 New Words   22

6 To Find Out More   23

7 Index   24

8 About the Author   24

Look closely.

Do you see the brown **leaves**?

An insect with wings is hiding there!

This insect is a moth.

It **spreads** its brown wings
to look like leaves.

7

Look closely.

Do you see the **branch**?

An insect is hiding there!

This insect is an inchworm.

It is shaped like a **twig**.

The inchworm looks like part of the branch.

Look closely.

Do you see the red **berries**?

A red insect is hiding there!

13

This insect is a ladybug.

It is red with black spots.

The ladybug blends in with
the berries.

14

15

Look closely.

Do you see the green leaf?

An insect is hiding there!

This insect is a grasshopper.

The grasshopper is as green as the leaf.

19

Which insect do you like the best?

21

New Words

berries (**bayr**-eez) small fruit that grow on bushes

branch (**branch**) the part of a tree that grows from its trunk

leaves (**leevz**) parts of a tree that grow from a branch

spreads (**spredz**) opens up

twig (**twig**) a small branch of a tree

To Find Out More

Books
How to Hide a Butterfly & Other Insects
by Ruth Heller
The Putnam Publishing Group

I See Animals Hiding
by Jim Arnosky
Scholastic

Web Sites
Most Wanted Bugs
http://www.pbrc.hawaii.edu/~kunkel/wanted/
This fun site has pictures and information about different bugs.
Find out which insects are the twelve most wanted!

Wonderful World of Insects
http://www.insects-world.com
Find out which of the world's insects are the biggest and smallest.

Index

berries, 12, 14

branch, 8, 10

grasshopper, 18

inchworm, 10

ladybug, 14

leaves, 4, 6

moth, 6

twig, 10

About the Author
Cate Foley writes and edits books for children. She lives in New Jersey with her husband and son.

Reading Consultants

Kris Flynn, Coordinator, Small School District Literacy, The San Diego County Office of Education

Shelly Forys, Certified Reading Recovery Specialist, W.J. Zahnow Elementary School, Waterloo, IL

Peggy McNamara, Professor, Bank Street College of Education, Reading and Literacy Program